DEDICATION

To Virginia
my best friend, the one making me whole.

You have blessed me with your love, understanding, strength and faith throughout the recall, research, and writing of this book. Thank you, my dearest Virginia, for making me a better person.

ACKNOWLEDGEMENTS

I wish to first and foremost thank God for being with me, guiding me, and gracing my life with wisdom and understanding.

My best friend Virginia who walks beside me every step of the way from poring through hundreds of hospital documents to envisioning success in helping little kids.

Numerous friends, co-workers, and family members encouraging, supporting, and praying for completion of this work as a tool for making life better for the lost and broken children in our nation.

I would also like to give a heartfelt thank you to honest and dedicated doctors, nurses, counselors, and staff members who truly salve and heal the wounds of little ones cast into the legal and social system.

This factual journey through my childhood is written with many prayers and divine guidance as a lantern of hope for the lost and often forgotten. My intent with this book is to promote awareness, well-designed solution, and positive change. In no way is this work a vengeful, vindictive assault against shadows of violence within my past. Rather, this is a testimony of gratitude to God for lessons learned, grace in understanding, and spiritual wisdom gained.

One evening while watching the nightly news on television, the lead item told of the arrest of a man in our neighboring town. Charged with abusing his small children, he had frequently put them in a barrel and closed the lid. His inane 'barrel' punishment would last for up to four hours at a time before finally releasing them.

This act of cruel and unusual punishment haunted me for days following the breaking news story. One sleepless night, I sat down and began to write my thoughts and heartfelt feelings on paper. How could this "Father" abuse his children in this atrocious manner? My heart hurt for the little ones. The result of venting my anger and frustration on paper was the birth of my poem "GOD BLESS THE LITTLE ONES"

The dun horse nickers softly as I lead him into the corral. Unbuckling the halter and turning him loose, I murmur, "Wish me luck, Cutter. Today is the day I start writing."

He gently nuzzles the brim of my hat, and I chuckle.

"I know I've already told you my life story. Now its time I tell folks who can and will help me protect other little kids."

My gaze slowly shifts upward toward the clear blue sky. Without warning, dark memories from times past return with a jolting clarity.

Numbing distress as the first blow from a hand or object slams against the small, terrified target. The door with its exterior lock leads into a small stark and dirty room void of windows. Fear draining life from the depths of a small child abandoned in an institution. The frantic fight for life as the plastic bag slowly destroys the breath of life. Overwhelming dread and fear from the prisoner seeing the armed guards, thick walls, and razor wire.

A tear slowly trickles down my cheek from remembrance, and I hear my low groan echo within the corral. Closing my eyes, I remove my hat and bow my head.

"Dear Heavenly Father, thank you. Thank You for this dawning of a new day with Your critters, the blue sky, the green grass, and Your love. Please help me to do Your work and make a positive difference in Your world. Amen."

Moments later, I enter the house. A suppressed sense of dread seeps into my soul as I walk up the stairs. Taking a deep breath and squaring my shoulders, I stride down the hallway to my office. Pausing at the door, I feel the determination of a strong and healthy man diminish into that of a small bruised and battered child. My heart rate increases, and I hear the latent fear pounding in my ears. My body weakens and knees nearly buckle as I slowly move across the room and sit in the chair behind the desk. A low groan echoes in the stillness with memories from the past pouring forth like a tidal wave. For a moment, time is frozen. I stare at the stacks of medical records, legal documents, old photographs, and letters covering the desktop.

A full minute passes before I pick up a card. It is the creation of a small child; a little one buried beneath legal lies in a state institution. The picture is that of a face, literally covered with large teardrops. The message inside the card is short and painstakingly written on colored construction paper.

I LOVE YOU, MOM . . . PLEASE DON'T BREAK MY HEART

John

My heart aches for that lost child still hidden from the world within me. My hands tremble as I put the card down and turn to the computer.

ONE

Hello. My name is John. Although bearing scars, both physical and emotional, I stand before you today, a strong and determined man of integrity and honesty, bowing my head in humble gratitude. In spite of atrocious and traumatic child abuse, God has blessed me with the precious gift of life.

Traveling back in time, I now expose my scars to society as proof of the need for positive action. I stand before you today a man determined to protect innocent kids from possible destruction wrought by vicious and emotionally unbalanced parents and a severely damaged social system.

From the moment of birth on December 21, 1977, my destiny lay hidden within the hands of a very emotionally unbalanced mother and a vicious, cold-hearted father in law enforcement. My mother was a tall woman, over six feet in height, and slender. My father was a bit shorter, but he was a stout-built, powerful man with a temper. Within a short time after my arrival into their world, they made it very clear that my conception was an accident and a regrettable mistake. Alcohol and drug abuse by my mother during pregnancy created a pre-maturely born and jaundiced infant with severe bouts of the colic. Thus, from the moment of my birth, my destiny lay in the hands of an angry, deceitful, and dangerous mother void of maternal love for me.

TWO

(Birth to age 5)

Physical and emotional pain was a natural part of life. I never felt the depth of a mother's devotion, a gentle touch of parental tenderness, or absolute unconditional love. Indeed, in abused children, these gifts from God are not missed . . . they simply do not exist!

Throughout my young childhood, emotions were narrow and negative. Dread and fear of impending pain overpowered any quiet moment of non-combatant treatment. If not being hit, kicked, or beaten, my body trembled and heart pounded with dread and fear as I waited for the onslaught to begin.

Photographs from infancy through young childhood reveal my life confined to a crib, most often bruised, battered, and sedated to the point of oblivion. Infrequent visits from grandparents on my father's side of the family offered a seldom and momentary reprieve from the parentally imposed abuse and solitary confinement. Fragments of memory from my first three years on earth reveal my mother tying a string or rope tightly around my private parts. The ensuing pain and damage from this atrocious abuse destroyed my ability to walk and, eventually even crawl. At this point, my mother forced me to sit in a chair for hours with an ice pack tucked between my legs.

Due to neglect and malnourishment, I was small for my age. When my siblings were present during assaults against me, Mother remained verbally silent. However, if she and I were alone, venomous words of hatred poured forth.

"I never wanted you in the first place!" she yelled as her weapon of choice slammed against my frail body. "Why were you born? I never wanted you!"

Her screams echoed through my soul as she rammed my head into walls or tossed me across the floor time after time. At times her rage against my presence on earth culminated in mashing lit cigarettes on the same area of my left hand. Even today, the scars from this repeated act remain visible and vivid.

"I never wanted you! I don't even like you!"

Unwarranted and unauthorized medications were more forthcoming than nourishing food. Shortly after ingestion of the pill given by my mother, the world slowed to a standstill as I slid into a state of immobility or unconsciousness.

"Swallow it, John! It will shut you up for a while!"

Under the care of my mother, bath time was a dreadful and pain-filled nightmare. Even my horrified screams did not prevent her from shoving me beneath scalding hot water in the tub.

Her voice sounded loud and high-pitched.

"I wish you had never been born!"

Anything at any given time could trigger her wrath against me. A disagreement with a sibling, an accidental spill, an angry word, or even a frown on my face sent her into a spasm of rage. Her fury unleashed in beating and kicking me before throwing me against the wall.

At some point, known only to my mother, the physical injuries and unwarranted drugs reached a plateau of absolute certainty of hospitalization. She would then put me in the car, seeking frantic and immediate help for her little frail boy with the unexplained injuries and mental disabilities.

Afraid to move or speak, I watched as my mother described my self-inflicted injuries to doctors and nurses. She was a master manipulator, turning each injury into a declaration of my severe mental disorder. Most times her tactics worked as we went directly from emergency rooms and into mental facilities. However, time after time, hospitals released me, stating there was nothing mentally wrong. After one hospital's release, they suggested using a point system to encourage positive behavioral patterns.

"Reward John with a point each time he does something good. When he has earned ten points, reward him with a gift."

My mother would smile and say, "I will do that starting immediately. I love my little boy and want the best for him."

Upon returning home, the point system went into effect . . . for a brief time. After receiving a little bar of soap carved into the shape of Darth Vader for ten points of good behavior, beatings, food deprivation, medications, and verbal abuse again replaced the point system.

One day my mom gave me large doses of medication and sat me in the bathtub. The drugs induced immediate paralysis. She then plugged the drain, turned on the water, and left the bathroom. I sat watching the water level rising but could not move a muscle. I truly believe God held my frail body in the upright position rather than allowing me to slide beneath the surface. As the tub overflowed and began pouring across the floor into other rooms, I heard my mom yelling.

"John let the bathtub run over!"

Sitting upright, unable to move, I watched her run into the room, stop and stare at me for a second. Then she jerked me from the bathtub and started beating me.

"You let that tub run over! I'm going to whip you black and blue! You are nothing but trouble. I am sick of looking at you!"

Indeed, intermittent trips to hospital emergency rooms became an ongoing part of life. Cold, brightly lit examination rooms, the strong scent of disinfectants, and the hushed sounds of bustling doctors and nurses became an almost daily part of my life. Perhaps to some in the outside world, I was an unfortunate, sickly child nurtured by a compassionate, caring mother.

THREE

Amid numerous trips to emergency rooms, there were infrequent times of questioning the cause of my injuries. With apparent suspicion from doctors and nurses arising, my mother hurriedly bundled me up and we left . . . to try a different facility with fewer questions. The outcome was either immediate hospitalization or ample prescriptions for sedatives to quell my waking moments and seizure medicine to mask the ongoing damages wrought upon my skull. Following my release from one hospital, I was unable to move for weeks. In retrospect, I am sure this immobility was due to drugs administered to me by my mother. My waking moments seemed a nuisance, and my existence a threat. Her private lifestyle was one involving heavy consumption of alcohol and late night partying. Numerous times, I was her greatest challenge regarding her social life. My siblings had friends with whom they could spend nights during her party times. However, I did not have friends. My life was in isolation at home or in institutions, void of fun-loving playmates and bonds of friendship.

"There's a party this weekend, and I'm going in spite of having to put up with you," my mom would declare as she stuck a pill in my mouth. "All I have to do is get rid of you!"

A moment later, the medication would drain my ability to defend myself. Shortly thereafter, we would enter another emergency room, followed by admittance into a mental facility. After reciting her charges of abnormal behavior against me and signing the legal papers, she would sadly smile at the admitting staff and gently touch my cheek.

"I love you. I'll see you later."

A staff member would take me from the room as my mother turned and left the facility.

During brief intervals at home, when only my mother and I were in the house, she removed my clothes and shoved me into the closet.

"Get out of my sight!" My mother's voice pierced through my being like a poison arrow. "I can't stand to look at you any more!"

Hours passed with me sitting huddled in a corner without food or water. Tears streamed down my face when I was no longer able to hold my bodily functions. Each time, I trembled and whimpered as the door flew open and my mother jerked me out of the closet. Every fiber in my naked little body felt the sting of pain as she beat me with an extension cord, belt, or whatever was handy for soiling on the floor. Traveling in the car did not offer a reprieve from abuse. My mom always had a bottle of Palmolive dish soap on the seat beside her. Filling my mouth with the green liquid insured silence and swallowing guaranteed immediate illness. She accomplished her objective either way.

One day I was with my dad in the car, and we were going over an overpass. I must have upset him somehow, and he stopped the vehicle. A moment later, I found myself outside of the SUV, and my dad was ramming my head into the fender. Time after time, I felt the throbbing pain as my skull smashed into the metal. Finally, he jerked me upright and threw me into the back of the vehicle.

Emotional abuse was a part of normal living; anything my mom could say or do to diminish my existence. At times, while loading groceries in the car, she picked me up and threw me into the trunk like one of the sacks. The inane disrespect was so natural that I did not question nor fight it. Indeed, no one was aware of this as I jumped out as soon as she opened the trunk to unload the groceries.

However, there is a time when even a terrified, bruised, battered little child instinctively knows his life is unbalanced and unfair. With the passage of time, simmering anger began building within my soul. Eruptions of uncontrollable rage poured forth, creating additional body slams against the walls and onto the floor. My defensive anger brought more torturous pain from extension cords, brooms, or other impromptu weapons. Fighting against the abuse increased my mother's wrath. She immediately countered with increased severity, and her parental punishment seared into my soul and tore at my flesh. During a severe beating, there was a point in time that my body no longer hurt. When this happened, my emotions erupted into unrestrained hysterical laughter. Perhaps this was my instinctive and unique method for maintaining the will to live. Although serving as a pressure release for me, the response merely intensified my mother's rage. The whipping escalated into banging my head against the floor, throwing me against the wall, and kicking me. Indeed, I stood alone in a vicious battle for survival.

FOUR

My father, although serving in a public position of authority to protect, was an angry and bitter man. Punishment incurred by his hand did not stop with severe spanking. His beatings ceased only after I fell to the floor in a state of unconsciousness. I was not allowed to get up in the mornings until my father was awake and out of bed. This rule resulted in occasional bed-wetting, which started my day in the throes of physical maltreatment at the hand of my father.

WUNSCHE SCHOOL
1983
(Age 5)

Enrolled in class for the first time, I attended Wunsche School, a private facility. One morning, my brother and I had a fight while I was getting ready to go. My mother called my father to come home and take care of his problem child.

My mom's voice sounded shrill and demanding as my dad answered the telephone.

"John is beating up his little brother! He is supposed to be getting ready for school. You come home right now and deal with him!"

My fear was unbearable torture. My heart pounded in my ears and body trembled as I waited for him. Although hoping for the timely arrival of the school bus to save me from a beating, it did not happen. All hope vanished as my dad thundered through the front door and grabbed me. Armed with a wooden spoon, a belt, a broom, and an extension cord, his powerful blows connected time after time against the tender flesh of this five-year-old boy. He beat me beyond blue. My body was black before he finally threw me against the wall. By the time he quit, the school bus had come and gone. He took me to school and left.

During first class, my body ached, and I stared at the black bruises on my arms. Feeling a sharp pain on one shin, I lifted my pants leg, silently checking the damage. Apparently, my teacher knew my fragile condition, and, a moment later, she took my hand and led me into the Principle's office. An immediate telephone call to Child Protective Services summoned further investigation. Moments after their arrival at the school, they took me to the restroom and removed my clothing. They took photographs of every part of my body from face to private parts to butt to back to legs. Every wound, scar, and deep bruise on my frail body exposed proof of abuse to the camera. Nevertheless, the proof of atrocious treatment changed nothing. My father was a police officer, and perhaps I was merely a small child needing a primary course in anger management.

Although unaware of the presence of Jesus in my life, I now know that He blessed me at that time with an ongoing miracle. I began to see visions, warning and preparing me with clarity in detail of forthcoming abusive situations. Awakening from the nightmarish dreams, my screams of terror echoed within the silence of the nights. Within a short time following each horror-filled vision, the scene soon became reality. Indeed, my nightmarish dreams literally came to life. The unexpected, unexplained warning, however, did not protect me from the onslaught of physical and emotional torture. I believe the visions were gifts from God, preparing and protecting me prior to another bout of cruelty. Within a vision, I saw the face of the bad person. I witnessed the upcoming abuse before feeling the agonizing pain within my body. The miracle from Jesus graced my soul with the promise of survival and an end to the beating.

The multiple and severe traumas inflicted on my skull from beatings by my mom and dad ultimately created seizures. Armed with reports from my mother that I had strangled our family dog with my bare hands, tried to drown my brother, severe aggression problems, having nightmares, and seeing visions, she laid the foundation for my admittance into an institution for the mentally disturbed. In reality, the little dog more than likely received the brunt of my mother's rage due to chewing on shoes and other things in the house. Small children often have disagreements and fights with siblings, and my siblings and I were no exception to this common behavior. It was true that my rage against beatings was building with each new onslaught of torturous punishment. Today I indeed thank God that the charge of 'seeing visions' was a statement of truth!

However, the day arrived when the accusations sealed my fate regarding removal from Wunsche School and admittance into Hermann Hospital, a facility for children with special needs. Perhaps it was during my commitment to this facility that serious marital problems between my mother and father culminated in divorce.

FIVE

Hermann Hospital
1983 - 1984)
(Age 5 – 6)

Indeed, I was a scared and lonely little kid with physical and emotional scars, but life in my abusive home was all that I had ever known. My heart ached with a powerful yearning to return.

Hermann Hospital, my new home away from home, was a unit consisting of four wings, about thirty-two rooms per wing, with the staff stationed in the center. I arrived on this scene at age five and daily routine in life was structured and predictable: the opposite from life at home. Each morning began with disbursement of medicine and breakfast followed by classes of arts and crafts. After lunch, there were therapy sessions, at times including tests with electrodes attached to my fingers. Instructed to identify various pictures, missed identification sent electrical shock waves through my body.

After supper, we watched television for a time, and had a snack prior to bedtime.

In quiet moments, however, tears streamed down my face as I looked out of my window, watching and waiting for my mom and sister to come to see me. My heart yearned for love, home, and siblings. At times, I felt sick at my stomach with loneliness. At times, I cried myself to sleep, and sometimes I washed tears from my face while brushing my teeth in the mornings. Each day I looked forward to mail call. Occasionally my grandmother sent me cards and gifts, but I never heard from my mother. Each time, with the last item of mail dispersed and nothing for me from my mom, my hopes faded into disappointment, a feeling of abandonment, and pain.

Within a short time, I developed a special trust and warm bond with one of my therapists. Her office was located in a wing across the facility from me. I was a little kid searching for kindness and often crawled on my hands and knees past the staff's station. When the coast was clear of foot traffic, I jumped up and ran to her office. This happened almost daily! Sometimes my uninvited visits even interrupted her scheduled sessions.

Infrequent visits from my family sent my heart soaring with happiness. For those few precious minutes, I felt the joy of kindness and love. But these infrequent moments were short-lived, thirty minutes, and bittersweet. My mom even left the impression that she truly cared about me. Although against the rules, she sneaked gum and candy from her pocket and gave it to me. When they left the building, I ran to the window, hoping I could see their car, but it was never within sight. Tears streamed down my face and my heart hurt with the void of not knowing when or if they would ever return. A promise of release was ongoing and always on the horizon two or three months in the future. Perhaps ten days prior to each release date, my discharge was postponed again . . . for another two or three months. This empty promise continued for nearly eighteen months before it became a reality.

The structured and protected life of Hermann Hospital was in sharp contrast with the uncertainty, pain, and abuse by my mom but it was the only home, environment, and life known to this little kid.

SIX

Following my discharge from Hermann Hospital and returning to family surroundings, all structured routines were gone. Daily chaos, cruelty, and beatings resumed. The one consistent moment in each day was my mom giving me a pill, and, moments later, the medication sedating me into a deep and abnormal sleep. Within a short time, I learned to put it under my tongue instead of swallowing it.

With angry eyes searing into my soul, my mother screamed, "Why aren't you asleep?"

In a fit of rage at my lack of obedience, she hid her intent by crushing the sedative into my food. After falling asleep at the table several times, I realized what she was doing and refused to eat.

Money was always in short supply in our family. Finances did not allow any funds for kid's treats. Rather, my mom combined water, sugar, and food coloring to serve as Kool Ade for us. She improvised popsicles, filling an ice cube tray with water and orange flavoring. One stick of gum served all four of us kids. One of us chewed it for a while, and then placed the wad in a corner of the freezer. The following day, another sibling chewed it before replacing it into the freezer. This routine continued through the four of us siblings until the precious tidbit was gone. Although loving one another, we were no different from any other little kids in a family. We did not always get along perfect. Unlike most families, however, there was never doubt about the one to receive the punishment. When disagreements occurred, I was the target for brash and severe discipline for these outbreaks, regardless of blame or circumstances. Settling fights between siblings and me resulted in beating on me with any handy object or calling my step dad home to carry out the punishment.

Each day included chaotic intervals of emotional and physical beatings, often followed by trips to emergency rooms and a probable possibility of confinement in facilities for the mentally and behavioral challenged. Time after time, my mother signed over my destiny to the Psychiatric Institute, a crisis center in Houston. I never knew what was going to happen or where I would be from one day to the next: at times from one minute to the next.

SEVEN

During my sixth year on earth, my mother had me admitted to the courts in Austin for a minimum of ninety days to exceed any length of time. Per their request, the state hospital could have been my home until they decided to allow me back into their lives.

AUSTIN STATE SCHOOL
(Children's Psychiatric Unit)
1984 – 1985
(Age 6 - 7)

This facility allowed thirty minutes visit from family members every two weeks . . . an eternity for a child. Thus, the light of youthful enthusiasm savored by the very young flickered and dimmed from the rejection. I did not understand the reason for taking me away from siblings and hidden in a strange foreboding building with strangers. My heart yearned for family acceptance, a gentle touch, a kind word, an encouraging praise, and love. At this time, Grandmother fought to gain full custody of me, but her protective and loving effort merely destroyed all communication with me as my mother placed a restraining order against her having any contact. This narrowed my familiar family world to two. My sister, who I dearly love, came with my mom each time. And, at the end of each thirty-minute visit,

I felt sick, lost, and abandoned as they again walked out of my life. Our time together was so short. Indeed, I was a little kid living with constant pain in my heart.

Austin State Hospital allowed me to telephone home twice per week, but, quite often, my mom did not want to talk to me.

Someone answered the phone, "Hello."

My heart raced with anticipation as I asked, "Is Mom there?"

"Who is calling?"

"John," I said. "Can I talk to Mom?"

After a brief pause, I heard, "She doesn't want to talk to you. Goodbye."

Tears streamed down my cheeks as the dial tone buzzed in my ear.

Thus, the refusal and silence replaced physical abuse. When finally hearing her voice on the phone, questions like, "How long are you going to leave me here?" or "When are you going to come up and see me?" poured forth. This cry for help brought me nothing but an echo of confusing hostility.

Several times my dad brought my grandfather and grandmother to the hospital, but the restraining order by my mother prevented their entrance into the building. Throughout my numerous relocations into various institutions, my grandmother always sent care packages to me. Her kindness and sweet love were the lifelines in my life. I could always count on her being with me in spirit and depend on her loving gifts to make me smile. However, during this time, our mutual love became a cruel weapon for my mother to inflict further pain upon me. Time after time, I stood at the window, watching my grandmother cry. It hurt so bad that I could not run and hold her and make her feel better. Throughout my young life, she was a nurse, but when off duty she was indeed the gentle one who truly loved and cared for me. Now, confined and alone, my heart yearned to put my arms around her and see her smile. But this was not to be. With each distant visit, tears streamed down my face and my heart felt broken as I waved from the window, watching them slowly return to the car and drive away.

This era in my life remains a dark, lonely, and frightening time within my mind, hidden . . . until now.

An average day at the Austin State Hospital (CPU) started with brushing my teeth, breakfast, and then attending class. However, education was limited to watching reruns of Dragnet, the teacher's favorite television show. Useful and enduring education was not available.

Abuse within the facility was plentiful with little or no reasoning behind it. Punishment was swift, severe, and frequent. Staff members used brute force, literally slamming us kids onto the floor. Two or three days in solitary confinement in an empty room without a bed and food remains vivid among memories of the months I spent there. Another form of discipline included the removal of the mattress on a Four Point Restraint bed, securing me to the metal rails and the bare springs. A staff member sat in the room, watching as other kids ran in, hit me, and ran back out.

Some things that happened did not make sense . . . even to me . . . a small child. A kid would pass out or fall down, and the staff would pick them up and carry them from the unit. Sometimes they brought them back, and sometimes I never saw them again.

Most mornings I awoke crying, hoping the nightmare would soon end. I blamed myself for not attending church with my grandparents and losing my temper too easily: not being a good boy!

Determined to correct my bad behavior, I started attending church regularly and walking a straight and narrow path to be that good little boy. However, my effort to please was seemingly unnoticed, and determination spiraled downward into defeat as conditions deteriorated.

One day a male nurse called me into the examination room. I immediately obeyed when he said that he needed to give me a physical checkup. He had me disrobe and explained that he was checking for different things. I obediently stood still as he fondled me. About thirty minutes later, he stopped, and I put my clothes back on. He then allowed me to leave the room. I returned to my dorm without telling anyone about the strange checkup.

A few weeks passed before the same staff member again called me into the room and repeated the previous treatment. Then he started calling me in every other week; then every week; and finally I knew when he was on duty, his thirty to forty-five minute "checkup" was a routine part of the day. Each time I returned to my dorm without telling anyone of the sexual abuse. The conditions of life were so bad in the facility that I just made up my mind to accept it as another thing that was going to happen that day.

This was my life for one year and one month in the children's division of the Austin State Hospital. As a child it was too painful to share, and as an adult I wanted to bury it forever . . . until now . . . this moment of true spiritual and physical healing.

EIGHT

The day finally arrived when I followed my mom through the Austin State Hospital exit door to freedom and family. Although happy and contented in being re-united with siblings, I was once again under the black cloud of pain and suffering wrought by my mother.

The perpetual and daily hits, kicks, and bashing, emotional trashing, and atrocious pharmaceutical misuse served as fuel for the embers of anger within my soul. My aggressive behavior increased. I soon learned that she had found a more powerful weapon to use against me. The new drug ingested with food, resulted in immediate immobility to move any part of my body . . . instantaneous, drug induced paralysis. My siblings witnessed my mom trying to force water in my mouth, which would have resulted in drowning. I was unable to swallow.

"Mom! Stop!" a sibling pleaded. "He can't swallow!"

In a calm voice, my mother replied, "John is thirsty. I am just giving him a drink."

Another time as I sat paralyzed, she attempted to feed me ice cream.

"Open your mouth, John. You like ice cream!"

"No, Mom," my siblings protested. "He can't swallow it."

As a little child who loved my mother and wanted to please, I did not know that her action and intent were deadly methods to remove me from her life.

Thus, after administering medication each time, a frantic mother entered an emergency room, clinging to her deathly ill child, pleading for instant admittance into the facility. Time after time, I found myself in the hands of doctors in the Psychiatric Institute, a crisis shelter, or in a strange hospital examination room. I never knew where I would be from one day to the next.

My nightmarish childhood memories are muddled and confused within my mind. The reality in details, dates, times, and test results, however, remain documented within hundreds of commitment and release forms now stacked on my desk. In looking through the paperwork, I find, among the torrent of short-term stays in various facilities, I was sent for a second internment in the Austin State Hospital at this time in my life. I again experienced the desolation of confinement in quarantine. The 'quiet room' was 8 x 10, with a mirror positioned in the corner, allowing the staff to see every inch of the interior perimeter. The walls and floor were concrete, and the thermostat was set at 61 to 62 degrees. The facility believed the colder temperature calmed the child. Memories of the four-point restraining bed void of the mattress once again became a reality. The overpowering feeling of helplessness returned as I was again strapped down for periods ranging from six to twenty-four hours without bathroom breaks. Even at this tender age, I tried to make sense of my life. I wondered what the future held for me, a child unable to stop or even partially control destiny.

Following my second release from CPU, I, again, was under the care of my mother.

With heightened pharmaceutical knowledge, she continued using the heavy drug that locked my muscles into instant paralysis. My mind remained clear, and I was fully aware of my surroundings and situation, but . . . I could do nothing to defend myself.

One evening she gave me the medication, but, rather than swallowing, I hid it under my tongue until she was not looking.

Although unaware at the time, I now know within my heart that Jesus directed and protected me from death at the hands of my mother that fateful night. I now know that His love gave me the courage to quickly and quietly remove and throw the paralyzing drug in the trash. However, I had to play the game of feigned immobility or get a beating, so I immediately faked paralysis. As usual, my mom picked me up and started toward the door.

"You kids stay here," she told my siblings. "I am taking John to the emergency room. I will be home as soon as I can."

She quickly carried me to the car and sat me down on the front seat. I was careful not to move a muscle. As the car moved forward, I silently wondered what facility I would be put into this time, and how long I would have to stay. Moments later, we were speeding down the road under the cover of darkness. This was not abnormal for us; a frantic and concerned mother in fear of her son's permanent paralysis. However, this time, was different . . . my muscles were not paralyzed by the drug. This time my entire concentration dwelled on faking the expected side affects. I knew I must play the game right or she would know . . . and I would get another beating. My heart pounded with fear, and I desperately tried to control my breathing so she would not notice anything different.

NINE

Seated in a frozen upright position beside my mother, we raced down the country road through the darkened night. Without looking directly at her, I saw my mom glance at me several times. It required every ounce of my concentration to avoid any movement from the bottom of my feet to the top of my head. The effort paid off as every muscle in my body remained taut and unmoving.

Suddenly she braked the car to a stop in an isolated area. As she got out and walked to the front passenger door, a cold wave of fear swept over me. We are not at a hospital! Or a house! I felt a strange and powerful terror rushing through my body. Instinct told me to run. No! I silently screamed! If I move any part of my body, she will know I didn't swallow that pill, and I'll get beat! I can't move! Stay stiff, John. Don't move. Don't even move your eyes!

Seconds later, she opened the door and jerked me out of the car, threw me onto the ground like a piece of trash, and pulled something from her pocket.

Even though I knew something terrible was happening, I did not move a muscle. She would really get angry if I moved!

Without saying one word, she slid a plastic bag over my head, covering my face. For a split second, my mind went numb.

I gasped for breath as her arm pressed tighter and tighter against the plastic bag covering my nose and mouth.

Suddenly the probability of death overpowered all fear of a beating. For the first time in my life, panic replaced all dread of violence and pain. Gasping and choking, my fingers clawed at the bag. My mom grabbed at my hands as she struggled to keep the plastic over my nose and mouth. My weak, undernourished body was no match against my tall, powerful, and very determined mother. Fighting for breath within the tomb of plastic, I felt her grip tighten even more against my face.

I struggled to open my mouth, allowing the plastic bag and the side of her arm to slide between my teeth. Closing my eyes and centering all of my strength into my jaws, I clamped down on her arm. As my teeth sank deeply into her flesh, she screamed with pain and immediately jerked her arm from my face. I leaped to my feet and tore the bag off my head. Tears of terror poured down my face as I ran blindly through the darkened night with heart pounding and fighting total hysteria.

I don't know how far I ran. Nor do I know where I stopped running. Exhausted, scared, and out of breath, I finally found a grownup who would be able to help me. I told him about my mother and her attempt to smother me. He looked at me and listened without saying a word. As I finally paused to catch my breath, he cleared his throat.

"You just stay with me, young fellow," he said in a soothing voice. "I will take care of you. What is your name?"

"John," I gasped. "My name is John Borgstedt."

"You just sit there and rest a minute, young fella'," he said. "You are safe now."

I nervously watched him walk to the desk and look in the telephone book before placing a telephone call.

He quietly talked to someone for a few minutes and then hung up. He looked at me and smiled.

"Okay, John," he said quietly. "Let's take a little drive, shall we?"

I sighed with relief and nodded my head. Within a very short time, he pulled into my mother's driveway and stopped the car. I felt sick at my stomach with dread and fear as I followed him toward the house. This homecoming was different from any I had experienced before. For the first time in my life, I knew that the abuse brandished by my mother now went beyond cruelty. A powerful and sharpened fear settled into my soul . . . my mother wanted to kill me!

She met us at the door and shook hands with the man. She hugged me and held me tightly in front of her as she smiled at the man who had brought her runaway son home. Her fingers dug into my shoulders as she talked to him.

"I am afraid John is a troubled little boy. I am trying to get help for him, but he often runs away." She hesitated and quietly added, "But this is the first time he has accused me of trying to kill him. I'm truly afraid his mental condition is getting worse. Thank you for bringing him home."

As she wiped away a forced tear, the man gently said, "That's okay, Mam. I hope you find help for John real soon. He seems like a nice little guy. I'm sorry he is having so much trouble."

This murder attempt was never mentioned again . . . except by my mother as a weapon for my future confinement in hospitals, institutions or a court of law. Our Heavenly Father knows the truth. He saved this eight-year-old boy from certain death by suffocation. He graciously strengthened my mind and frail body to survive.

TEN

Shortly after the fateful night of the murder attempt, life returned to normal for me with heavy medication and routine beatings. However, kids have a special gift for discovering unexpected and exciting adventures. My siblings and I were no different. Such was the case the day after a vacant house nearby caught fire!

One of my siblings and I decided to explore the damaged building after the Fire Department left the scene. The scent of charred wood, black soot and ashes captivated our senses of adventure. Combing through the remains felt like we were two brave explorers, seeking treasure within the dangerous woodlands. Indeed, we cut a wide and wild path through the mysterious remnants of the old burned building!

Within a short time following our venture, the Sheriff arrived at our house. He told my mother that my fingerprints were at the scene of the fire.

*I*mmediately, I was sitting on a chair in the living room with my mother standing beside it, daring me to deny the sheriff's accusation of arson.

For nearly five hours, over and over I heard,

"You did it! Why don't you just admit it? You started that fire and burned the house!"

During the first two or three hours of the interrogation, I just quietly denied the accusations. Knowing in my heart that I was telling the truth, the grownups, even my mom, could not force me into a false confession.

Nevertheless, the Sheriff and my mom were relentless. I was tired, thirsty, hungry, and emotionally beaten when, in the fifth hour, I murmured, "Yeah. I did it."

Due to the extended and multiple commitments in hospitals and mental facilities, I did not know how to write my name. Formal and normal education had not been a part of my life. Therefore, exhausted and defeated by the determined accusers, I made my legal mark on a confession to a charge of arson.

Consequently, my mother loaded me into the car for another trip to an emergency room, followed by admittance into another facility.

DEPELCHIN HOME
1985 – 1986
(Age 7 - 8)

In the fall of 1985, my mom had me admitted into the DePelchin Home, which was a minimum-security facility for troubled and special needs children. The school was a step up from prior schools, providing rooms with closets. A volleyball court, basketball nets, and swings were readily available for recreational purposes. Indeed, my life, once again, settled into a normal daily routine.

One of my counselors became an important and special part of my life during this time. She cared about me as a little person . . . not just as a patient. With kindness and patience, she taught me the basic art of tying my shoelaces, writing my name, and finally graduating to writing my name in cursive. Coming on duty, she often brought me little gifts of toys or candy. Her gentle and caring attitude remains a warm memory within me today.

One morning I heard a familiar voice calling my name. Turning toward the sound, I saw my dad enter the back of the building and walk up the hallway toward me.

"Let's go, John," he said.

In a bit of shock, I asked, "Where are we going?"

"To play Putt Putt Golf," he stated as though this was nothing out of the ordinary.

Following him out of the building, I felt elated that my dad wanted to spend time with me.

"You have to sign me out, Dad. You need to tell them you are taking me with you."

He did not even slow his pace as he said, "I'm not telling anybody anything."

"But – But – they will think I've been kidnapped!"

The mixed emotions of happiness in being with my dad and the fear of punishment for not signing out caused my heart to pound in my ears as we left the building. However, arriving at the car, the dread of impending trouble for leaving vanished for a time when I saw my grandmother and stepmother waiting for me. Indeed, this is a warm memory of family fun even though a cloud of fear remained with me throughout our day together. My mind kept repeating, If only my father had signed me out . . . ! However, upon returning I found that my counselor friend had covered my absence by reporting that I was with her in class all afternoon. She will forever remain a special blessing of kindness and caring in my heart.

Months later, released from DePelchin and placed back into the custody of my mother, I returned home. Upon arrival, I learned that I had a step-dad and a newly constructed bedroom next to the garage. It was a segregated entity, entirely separate and a distance from the house. The new addition had one door and no windows or bathroom. It was just one small barren and dark room. The one door was equipped with a reverse lock, barring even emergency exit. The barren and bleak interior contained a bed, sheets, blanket, coffee can and milk jug to serve as a toilet, my clothes, and a radio. The enclosure, specially constructed under the supervision of my mother, had extra insulation, plus egg cartons, which insured the room to be entirely soundproof.

I stood in the room beside my mother in stunned silence as she folded her arms and glared down at me.

"You are going to school and when you get out of school, you will come straight home and go to this room and stay until time to go back to school! You will not eat with the rest of us. You will not sleep in the house with the rest of us. And you will not have play time with my other kids. Do you understand?"

I wanted to scream 'No!', but I looked down at the floor and nodded my head. Thus was my homecoming back into life in the 'real' world.

Soon I was attending Wunsche School once again. However, at home, my stint of solitary confinement was just beginning. No longer allowed to play or even eat meals with my siblings, my mother handed a peanut butter and jelly sandwich or a bowl of cereal laced with medication through the door. When able, my sister sneaked extra food into the "quiet" room. The solitary confinement added fuel to the raging fire of frustration mounting within me. I spent many hours alone in the 'quiet room', pacing, defensively kicking and hitting at the shadows of pain, frustration, torment, and loneliness. Even at eight and nine years of age, I tried to make sense of my life, but the attempt merely added fuel to my anger.

Minimal moments out of the 'quiet room' thrust me back into the clutches of chaos. My mom always found a reason to ram my head into the wall, throw me on the floor, and kick me. The abuse was never-ending. Time after time, I was in the car with my mother going from one emergency room to another facility. My life was indeed a perpetual state of the unknown, and yet always with the same result. Following each release, I returned to her beatings, emotional cruelty, drugs, and solitary confinement in the 'quiet room'.

Frustration, anger, and finally rage ravaged my soul. I threw the drug-laced sandwiches against the wall or tossed them in a corner. As hours slipped into days, the stench from body waste and decaying food became a haven of filth for hordes of cockroaches and other vermin. I was a boy lost in a black hole of degradation, dishonor, and hate without a compass for direction, a mentor for leadership, or a lantern for love and hope.

ELEVEN

I accepted the attention of pain and abuse as a routine part of the day. However, one afternoon my mom slugged me, knocking me to the floor, and I stood up to face her. My body trembled with rage as I glared at her.

Suddenly hysterical, I started screaming, "You want me dead! Okay, Mom, I will kill myself! That should make you happy! I will do it! I will just kill myself!"

She grabbed me, and, within minutes, we were in another emergency room. I covered my face in my hands to avoid the accusing stares from my mother and doctors as she described my insane behavior.

"John is crazy," she said. "He is even telling people that I tried to kill him. He is a constant threat against me and his siblings."

She paused only a moment before pleading her final request,

"My son needs help. John is suicidal! He has to be admitted into the hospital now! I couldn't take it if something bad happened to him!"

Years of intimidation and cruelty had stolen any chance or courage to defend myself against her accusations. With an aching heart and feeling sick at my stomach, I stared at the floor and said nothing.

With paperwork soon signed, sealed, and my fate delivered back into the hands of Hermann Hospital, my mother turned to me and smiled.

"John, you be a good boy. Just try to get better, okay? I love you." Slipping her purse strap over her shoulder, she added, "I'll see you later."

A staff member put his hand on my shoulder and said, "He will be fine. Won't you, John. Come with me. We will get you settled in your room."

The sound of my footsteps on the tile floor echoed against memories of similar journeys through similar surroundings and circumstances. Little did I know, Hermann Hospital was merely a six-day stopover on a journey into a re-occurring nightmare.

HERMANN HOSPITAL
TEXAS MEDICAL CENTER

Name of patient: Borgstedt, John
Unit #84-17117-2
Date of Admission: 8/25/87
Date of Transfer: 9/2/87

History of present illness: This is the second Hermann Hospital admission for this nine-year-old white male brought in by his mother after threatening to kill himself and after threatening her. This patient admitted to hitting his mother after she hit him, and stated that he said in anger that he would kill himself just to show her. He denies any desire to hurt himself at the time of this interview.

Past Psychiatric History: Hermann Hospital, 1984, old chart presently not available. Austin State Hospital School 1984 – 1985. He was there for one year and two months. DePelchin Home 1985 – 1986, released in September 1986. Mother states she was told he was too violent to stay there and has lived at home ever since.

Social History: He lives with his mother and stepfather. . . . This is the third marriage for the mother, and by history through the therapist, his mother's relationships have been very chaotic to the family structure.

The mother also states . . . eating . . . describes him as picky. She states that his sleep was disturbed for some time, but seems to have been fairly stable lately. She cannot describe any other - -- - - - negative symptoms at this time.

Medications on Admission: Imipramine 25 mg bid. 50 mg. HS, and Tegretol 300 mg. qam. , and 400 mg. qpm and HS.

Hospital Course: During hospitalization, patient was noted to make suicidal and homicidal threats when he became angry. Recommendations were made for long-term treatment at Austin State Hospital with an OPC and 96-hour letter filed. Preliminary hearing was to be with the court although the mother decided that John did not need to see the judge, and she waived the court hearing.

. . . When told that he would be going to Austin State Hospital for long-term treatment and evaluation, he became tearful. His behavior improved while on the ward during the several days hospitalization with less acting out on the unit. During group session on two days prior to admission, John spent the majority of his time on working on a letter to the judge in charge of his case, that TL025 #7711. . . . His mother waived the court hearing and agreed to commitment upon recommendation for long- term treatment at Austin State Hospital.

I felt like I was in a nightmare and couldn't wake up. My stomach hurt, and my heart pounded with dread and fear of the future. Memories of the four-point restraint bed without a mattress, solitary confinement, and physical punishment from the staff poured forth.

TWELVE

Heartache, anger, and dread hung over me like a shroud as the car came to a stop at the entrance.

"Please, Mom, I don't want to stay here," I said. "I don't like this place."

Without saying a word, she gathered the paperwork given by the attending physician in Hermann Hospital and stepped from the car. My legs felt so weak that I stumbled and almost fell down before regaining my balance and following her. I tried to hide my trembling hands as I sat down in a chair in the corner of the admittance office. I tried not to listen as she described me as a psychotic child and a true danger to siblings. After signing a number of documents, she smiled and stood up. A moment later, she hugged me and said,

"I love you, John. I'll see you later."

Then she was gone.

AUSTIN STATE HOSPITAL
(CPU)

John C. Borgstedt #095366
Date of Admission: 9/2/87
Date of Evaluation: 9/14/87

Relevant History: John is a 9 – ½ year-old boy with a long history of abuse, neglect, institutionalization, and aggressive behavior. He has also been diagnosed with having a seizure disorder, and during the past year was unconscious . . . " While he appeared to be of average intelligence and demonstrated considerable cooperation and concentration throughout this testing session, his classroom performance remains at a first grade level . . . indicative of a boy who has experienced severe emotional traumata, who feels alone, insecure, and isolated from his family, and is prone to sense his own incompetence, with resultant . . .

Bitter tears streamed down my face each morning when I awoke. An average day included seeing kids slammed onto the floor by a staff member, and, too many times to recall, I was that kid. Cruelty against young patients was a way of life within this facility.

Although speaking the truth, I quickly found out that mentioning I would rather be dead brought severe repercussion. Putting me in a room by myself, they took all of my clothes, put me in a paper gown, and locked the door. Confinement remained intact until I disclaimed all notions of suicide and death. Doctors, nurses, and staff often referred to my aggressive behavior as 'acting out'. However, in my world, I was merely surviving with the methods and attitude bestowed upon me by my role model mother. If anyone entered my space, I fought like a caged animal, protecting myself against further exploitation. The result was numerous stays in solitary confinement in a small room void of a bed or mattress. Each 'lock up' would be a two or three day stay without food.

Months later, following a second release from the Austin State Hospital (CPU), I, once again, returned home to confinement in my 'quiet room'. One evening, in a burst of rage, I kicked the door, striking the knob. My heart pounded with fear as it fell to the floor. I knew this would mean another beating, another trip to the emergency room, and yet another admittance into an unknown facility. While trying desperately to replace the doorknob, I accidentally opened the door. Again, my heart raced until realizing the knob did not appear broken when stuck back in place. I had accidentally found an escape route hidden from my mother.

From that moment in time, every night I waited until everyone in my family was asleep. As the world slept, I silently slipped into the night for a brief taste of freedom without perpetual abuse. This was my time for raiding the pantry for food. It was my quiet time of looking at the world through the eyes of a small innocent child. A child forced to hide within the safety and darkness of night.

Following the attempted murder at the hands of my mother, fear for my life became an integrated part of my being. Anger, confusion, and the ever-present, ever-increasing emotional and physical abuse surfaced like volcanic lava late one night. After everyone was asleep, I removed the broken doorknob and slipped out of the filthy, roach infested 'quiet room'. My body felt numb, and my mind seemed calm and clear as I silently walked into the kitchen. Opening a drawer, my fingers tightened around the knife handle. It felt sturdy, strong, and right in my hand. Although not yet ten-years-old and my body scarred, bruised, and malnourished, I felt in control of myself for the first time. My thoughts seemed clear and right as I slipped down the hallway toward my mother's bedroom. If my mother is gone, I will never be slammed into the wall or hit or kicked or choked, scalded, or smothered again. I will not be taken to emergency rooms and put in hospitals.

I put my hand on the doorknob of her bedroom. It was locked. I heard a sound behind me and turned around. My sister was looking at me.

"John," she whispered. "What are you doing with that knife?"

For the first time, I realized that I was about to do something very wrong. The knife would have stopped my mom's terrible beatings, the horrible drugs, the crazy trips to emergency rooms, different institutions, physical and emotional pain. The knife would also end my mother's life! Shock and fear of my intent stopped me in my tracks. I dropped the knife and ran from the house and back into the 'quiet room'.

Indeed, the passage of time granted me the insight to know that God used my sister as my guardian angel. Since that fateful night, I do understand and know in my heart that even a small child has a breaking point. The yearning desire for love, peace, kindness, and acceptance can become a raging demand, regardless of cost.

Realizing the depth of danger in my actions, my sister told my mother about my strange behavior with the knife. The result of my intent to do bodily harm sealed my fate.

AUSTIN STATE HOSPITAL
CHILDREN'S PSYCHIATRIC UNIT

(6/24/88)
John Borgstedt (d.o.b.) 12/21/77 #095366
Date of re-admission: 06/24/88

INFORMANTS: "Bonnie Rogers, mother, provided pertinent update information preceding John's readmission . . . John got into a fight with peer, initiated a headlock on him and tried to break his neck . . . increasingly aggressive behavior, which included setting fire to a vacant house . . . He threatened to kill his mother and threatened to kill himself . . . Inappropriate sexual behavior with animals as well as with other children . . . His only consistent relationship has been with his mother, who remains steadily supportive of John in her attempts to obtain help for him . . . "

Thus, months passed with the same nightmarish cruelty, isolation, and emotional upheavals as before in the Austin State Hospital. Finally, the day arrived for my release into the custody of my mother and another stepfather. It was yet another return to beatings, high-powered drugs, and isolation in the 'quiet room' . . . indeed, Home as I knew it.

THIRTEEN

One afternoon my mom unlocked the door of the 'quiet room', and said, "Come out here, John. The Sheriff wants to talk to you."

I walked outside. The officer glared at me, and I shifted my attention to my feet.

Before he could say a word, my mom said, "I will get his meds and clothes, so you can take him."

"Whoa, wait a minute," the Sheriff responded. "I just want to take John down to the station and talk to him for a while. Somebody started a fire near the school. And since John has a record for arson, I think we need to talk to him."

I knew nothing about the fire at the school. I was neither afraid nor dreading to go with the Sheriff.

However, innocence did not protect me from long and grueling hours of interrogation by my mother and the Sheriff. Time after time and hour after hour, I repeatedly denied any knowledge of the fire at the school. Finally, exhausted emotionally and physically, I laid my head on the table.

"All you have to do," the Sheriff said, "is sign this paper."

He laid a written confession on the table.

I looked at him and my mom and said, "But I didn't do it."

"We are going to stay right here until you admit to arson."

Sometime later, I signed the confession. Another sheet of paper was slid onto the table in front of me.

"What's this? I said I did it! Can't I go now?"

"This is to say that we didn't coerce you into admitting anything. Sign it, and this will all be over."

I signed.

Within a short time, my case was before the Texas Youth Commission in Houston, Texas. I was facing the serious charge of arson. Records and testimony from my mom and signed confessions indicated this was the second time for this type of illegal conduct. Prior to going before the judge, I relaxed a bit as I met my attorney. He smiled and patted me on the shoulder.

"Don't be scared, John," he said. "I have been appointed to represent you. Don't worry, Son. I will be right beside you and help you."

I looked up into his face. Slowly nodding my head, I smiled. The first ten years of my life had been a constant battle for survival, and I fought it alone. This time I would be standing beside someone who would fight for me.

Nothing or no-one, however, had prepared me, an innocent child, for facing a Judge and a court of law. The room was big and intimidating with hard chairs, stark tables, and the ominous looking judge seated above everyone else. Whispering voices echoed against the heavy wood and high ceiling. My grandparents, mom, and appointed attorney sat at a long table when I entered. Fighting back tears, I sat down beside my grandmother. I glanced at my attorney who had assured me that he was with me and would help. However, he chose to sit in a chair on the other end of the long table. I looked at my grandmother, and she gently patted my arm. I gulped and tried to smile as the attorney's words of encouragement echoed in my mind.

"I will be with you. Don't be afraid. I will be right there beside you."

Seated beside my granny and looking at my attorney, I took a deep breath.

"All rise!" a voice boomed. "Judge . . . ."

I stood up and looked at the Judge. Suddenly I felt even smaller and more vulnerable than usual, and my gaze shifted downward. It didn't seem so scary if I didn't look at him.

Soon I heard my name called within the large intimidating room. My heart pounded in my ears as I sat down and glanced at the man who said he was going to help me. He did not look at me. He opened a notebook of some kind and seemed to be reading it. I glanced at Granny again, and she tried to smile.

A moment later, my history of mental instability followed a barrage of accusations of bad behavior. Words like threatening siblings, arson, uncontrollable rage, animal cruelty, abnormal sexual conduct, suicide, attempted murder, and habitual runaway painted a bleak portrait of me. I looked at my attorney at the opposite end of the table, but he did not look at me. Nor did he say one word in my defense. My heart pounded with anger. He was not saying one word to help me! He was just sitting there . . . Saying nothing! Doing nothing! I felt shock and rage burn through my body and mind. My attorney, my mom, my grandparents, and I watched and listened as the judge rendered his decision . . .

"You have been found guilty of arson, for the second time, plus numerous other charges of misconduct, young John Borgstedt. You are sentenced to a minimum of three hundred sixty five days in TYC (Texas Youth Commission), but not to exceed your eighteenth birthday."

I looked at my attorney. He did not say one word in my defense. He just stood at the long table that looked like The Lord's Last Supper, facing the judge's bench . . . saying nothing! Doing nothing!

As the sentence echoed against the silence of the courtroom, my granny got up and walked to the other end of the table. She quietly questioned my attorney. Anger exploded within me as the attorney shrugged his shoulders. Although a little boy small for my age, I stood up and shouted,

"Why didn't you say anything?" My body trembled with anger as I sputtered, "I thought you were going to help me! I didn't start that fire!"

My attorney glared at me and growled, "Sit down!"

The judge slammed his gavel down.

"Order!" he demanded. "Order in the court! Take your seat, young man!"

I spat toward the judge and screamed, "Screw you! You won't let me talk, and my attorney isn't saying anything to help me! I didn't start any fire! I didn't do anything wrong! You are telling me how much time I have to do, and I don't have anything to say about it?"

My body was shaking with fury as I spit at the judge. Immediately placed in custody, the officer started leading me toward the side door of the courtroom. With tears in their eyes, Granny and Papa hugged me. My mom looked at me and said, "I love you. See you later."

Looking over my shoulder, I watched as she turned and left the courtroom. Indeed, she left court as the victor in her final crusade to crush me. I was ushered into a holding cell, and the door clanged shut behind me. It would be the last time I would see my mom until I reached age twenty-two.

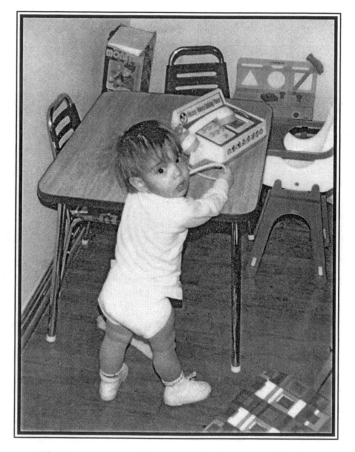

*This is a picture of me as a little guy in the first
institution that my mom put me in.*

Austin State Hospital in 1986 (we were sharing one of the very few happy moments together).

First grade. I was 7 years old at
Old Concord Elementary School.

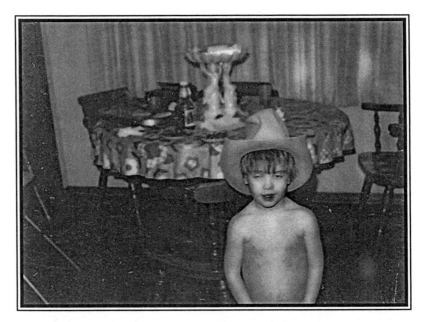

This is a picture of me with my grandfather's hat on.
This was one of the many days where my mother had me doped up
with too much medication.

Me as an infant with those cute little dimples.

Jan 1985. My mother brought me a birthday cake.
I was in Austin State Hospital.

This is a picture of my granny and I.
She came to visit me at Corsicana Boys Home.

This is a picture of me and my grandfather.
He came to visit me at Corsicana Boys Home.

This is a picture of my mom.
This shows her state of mind—very alone, very depressed.

FOURTEEN

The Psychiatric Institute of Fort Worth was at the top of the line in comparison with prior admissions in other facilities throughout my life. Staff members were truly kind and nice: caring about us physically and emotionally. The food, served buffet-style, was tasty, hot, and very well prepared. The Institute had beneficial therapy sessions conducted by true professionals who cared. During this time, I sent an ongoing chain of letters, cards, and drew pictures for members of my family, expressing my love for them. I love you, Mom . . . Please don't break my heart was among them. Compassionate staff members worked very hard to keep my mind busy and off my mother. I shared a room with a roommate, and we had a thermostat to regulate the temperature. We had our own bathroom and personal locker with drawers. In the hallway of the facility, a board listing all of our names honored good behavior with a point system. Upon reaching higher levels of the point system, your rewards increased. High points offered field trips to play Putt Putt Golf and other fun excursions. This was my temporary home for six or seven months before they transferred me to a correctional facility for unwanted children as ordered by the judicial system.

CORSICANA BOYS HOME
Cottage 11
(1987 – 1990)
(Age 10 - 13)

Cottage Eleven was the established housing and supervision for the younger unwanted children. The staff was nice and caring, and the caseworkers really looked out for me. If I did something wrong, the counselor on duty would say, "Okay, John. I am going to give you one more chance." I am grateful that their 'one more chance' was offered quite often over the following three years. They knew my prior hospitalization history and recorded physical and mental abuse, and honored me with patience and understanding.

Counselors and other staff members made sure that each holiday was a special time for me. Individuals lovingly accepted me into their family's celebration for Halloween, Thanksgiving, Christmas, and Easter. Each time, my host made sure that I felt wanted and loved in their traditional homes for the special occasion. This precious gift of kindness granted me insight into family loyalty, love, sharing, and caring. Joining them for brief intervals showed me that love for one another does not hurt.

The kids of Cottage 11 celebrated Christmas with the same spirit, excitement, and enthusiasm as those in traditional family homes. The counselor told each of us to make a ten-item Wish List for Santa. Then, they wanted us to choose four alternatives for each of the ten. As we were kids who had nothing, our wish list consisted of basic and needed items rather than frivolous toys. Christmas Eve, Santa arrived with a big trailer full of presents for us. On Christmas Day, we all sat down and feasted on a huge dinner with all the trimmings.

Each year, they celebrated my birthday, complete with my choice of the cake, gifts, and special attention. Indeed, this time in Cottage Eleven was as close as I ever got to a normal childhood.

At times, I thought of my mom and wondered what she was doing and if she missed me. These moments became less frequent with the passage of time. As days, weeks, and months passed, my only family members who came to visit were Granny and Papa and Grandma and Grandpa, my grandparents on both sides of the family. Grandma often sent care packages of Granola bars and Trail Mix; snacks good for me, which instilled a loving taste for them that I continue to enjoy today. Time spent with grandparents erased all loneliness for a while.

During my Cottage Eleven days, unlike me, kids came and kids left. It was a permanent home to me, and I became the campus favorite among staff members and co-residents. The counselors and other ladies working there, loved me more than my mom did, and when they were transferred or quit, I felt a personal loss.

During this period in my life, my gift of premonitions was very active. One night I dreamed a cottage burned. The vision was unclear on which cottage, and I awoke with a dread of my residence consumed by fire. I wrote down the details of the dream and shared the vision with others.

As usual, the dream became a reality. However, the casualty was Cottage Ten that burned to the ground. A resident had started a fire in the laundry room, and the flames spread over the entire building. Receiving a vision of upcoming problems, often created friction. I tried to avoid the unfolding situation by acting out.

"John," a staff member said in a firm voice. "You are supposed to be helping Tony! Get in there and help him!"

The memory of my dream washed through my mind. Tony was calling me names, taunting me into a fight. Finally, I lost my temper and flew into a rage. After several exchanged punches, I was sitting on top of him, pounding on his face.

The staff member repeated, "Get in there and help Tony!"

I shook my head and said, "No. I don't want to."

Understandably, disobedience was unacceptable and not tolerated. My dream once again became a reality.

Similar circumstances occurred quite often, which resulted in harsh, not cruel, reprimands. Refusals to obey never worked, and my visions always became reality.

God also blessed me with a keen instinct in determining the character of a person. It seemed that I knew which people to avoid, and which ones were safe to trust. Thus, life was abnormal but safe, routine, and stable for three years.

Throughout this three-year period at Corsicana, I had tried telephoning home many times. At first, no one would answer the phone, and finally a recorder informed me that the number was no longer in service. At this point, I totally lost contact with my family. It was hard, but with time, I adjusted to this loss as an unpleasant fact of life. However, my aggressive behavior did not subside. Although hidden deep within my heart, the inner rage I carried throughout early childhood continued to explode all too frequently.

FIFTEEN

Cottage Eleven was a home for little kids. Upon reaching age thirteen, I was transferred to Cottage Fourteen, which was housing for teenagers. This move was hard for me. I had survived and grown emotionally while under the care of accepting personnel and peers, but this was not the case with new co-residents and staff. My days of walking to the front of the line in the cafeteria, getting two cartons of milk, and special attention from the staff, without consequence were over. In this Cottage, I was the 'new kid on the block' and had to earn acceptance and respect. My reputation as campus favorite among Cottage Eleven staff members and residents branded me with immediate rejection. The teenagers were much older, the staff determined to put me down a notch, and the atmosphere more aggressive. The process of acceptance and establishing my position with peers took over a year to achieve.

Corsicana was a big facility, housing many kids. Besides schoolroom classes, sports were an important part of the school curriculum. Softball and basketball tournaments were large and exciting events with rewards for the winners taken on special field trips. Sometimes we were given a full day of playing Putt Putt Golf or going to Pancho's for dinner. The first time I went to Pancho's I felt I had died and gone straight to heaven! It was 'all you can eat' buffet with every kind of food imaginable, and we all ate until we hurt and loved every minute of it!

At Christmastime, Mr. Barnaby, a prominent businessman, took every child living on the entire Corsicana campus to the Holiday Inn for dinner. He paid the staff to work overtime to fix all of the food we wanted to eat. We went wild ordering whatever we wanted and tasting some of every dish available. Indeed, Corsicana holds some very good memories for this banished child cast into the depths of the legal system.

However, at age fifteen, my life once again took a dramatic turn into new and frightening territory. I truly believe God forewarned me with another vision of the danger lying ahead.

One night I dreamed that I was standing at my window looking outside. It seemed that I was looking down a hill at a tall fence. Strands of razor wire glistened in the sunlight on the top of the high enclosure. I awoke with dread and fear pounding in my heart.

One month later, a transfer to Gainesville State School turned my world upside down. While being led through the facility to my quarters, I felt the icy stares of hatred pouring from the kids. Later, standing at my window, I suddenly realized that I was looking down a hill at a high fence with razor wire along the top glistening beneath the sunlight . . . my vision was once again a reality.

Gainesville State School was a facility housing juvenile murderers, drug pushers, and armed robbers: young, hardened gang members and criminals. Prior to this incarceration, I had not heard of the Crypts or Bloods or the Hispanic gangs like the East Side 13. It was a shock for me to see kids with tattoos and wearing bandanas representing their gang affiliation.

The staff was working for a paycheck and taking the side of least resistance at the first sign of trouble. They were afraid of these kids. I, as a non-gang member, a loner, and a newcomer was the main target for aggression from all of them.

One morning I stepped into the cafeteria and glanced toward a gang member. He saw me looking at him and slowly stood to his feet. Everyone else at the table also stood up. I quickly diverted my gaze and tried to walk to the food line. In a flash, they jumped me. Fists pounded on my face, and boots crashed against my chest, groin, and legs as I hit the floor. Seconds later, they left me, beaten and bloody, and returned to the table. A minute later, three staff members picked me up and carried me to the infirmary. The damage to my jaw was so extensive I had to drink and eat through a straw for a time. The staff put me on report and sent me to security as punishment . . . the 'safe' path for the staff.

This facility was a perpetual round of kids molesting kids, staff molesting kids, teachers molesting kids, and the staff punishing the innocent to diffuse all situations and avoid gang member attacks against them.

Throughout this nightmare, I asked myself, "What did I do to deserve this?"

In searching for this answer and craving illusive hope for a better life, I faithfully attended church. My grandmother had insisted that I attend Catholic Mass with her in the past, and I truly needed that connection now. Even this effort failed to produce the peace that I so desperately needed and wanted. Exhausted emotionally and physically beaten, I decided to end my life. Drinking chemicals from the horticulture class to accomplish this did not work. In fact, the attempt made life worse as they took away all of my clothes, replacing them with a paper gown. Locked in a room by myself, I was restricted to a liquid diet for weeks. Heavy doses of medication brought back memories of the treatment inflicted upon me by my mother, and this combined with the solitary confinement merely made me worse.

Finally realizing that life would never improve if I did not lie, I told doctors I did not want to die. I was better and ready to face life again. It worked, and I returned to daily living among the gang members and heartless staff.

I honestly do not know to this day, why I was sent to Gainesville State School to be detained with hardened delinquents. Thoughts and dreams of going home had died long ago. I now wanted to return to Corsicana where I had spent the most stable and healing part of my life.

During this time, I went to a psychologist for counseling every week. I was losing all perspective and knew it. Time after time, he suggested putting me on anti-depression medication.

"I am not depressed! This is not the place for me," I insisted. "I'm not like these people. I'm not a killer!"

After many sessions like this, he apparently agreed and assisted in getting me transferred to a more suitable and stable facility. I felt relief pour over me as I walked through the gate and left the razor wire glistening atop the high fence behind me. However, the scars, anger, and aggressive behavior remained deeply embedded within my heart and soul.

SIXTEEN

The previous fifteen years of my life had taught me to survive, regardless of obstacles and opposition. My attitude was defensive and aggressive, and my body now larger and strong enough to support both. With this combination, my future remained a scary, unstable, and dangerous rollercoaster, twisting and turning every few weeks. They sent me to Texas Key in Houston. This facility was a large house in a bad part of the city. Here, too, I lived with gang members and an in-house, incompetent staff. Drugs were prevalent in this neighborhood and through the facility. Food was in constant demand as the staff most times took it to their homes or ate it while on duty. I was in trouble daily for sneaking into the freezer for food or taking extra snacks. Fighting had become a normal and daily part of my life, be it with other kids or staff members.

Unhappy, emotionally shell-shocked, and in constant trouble for fighting and stealing food, I ran away without a plan, destination, or forethought. A short distance from the house, I hid in some bushes. For a time, I watched people walking the streets and driving by searching for me. Finally, I curled up on the ground and slept.

I did not know that the facility had notified my mother that I was missing, and she had telephoned the police. She informed them that I was a dangerous runaway and going to kill her. An All Points Bulletin was immediately issued for my arrest.

The following morning after borrowing a quarter from a stranger, I telephoned back to Texas Key and spoke to the lady in charge, asking if I could come back.

"If you will come back right now, John," she firmly stated, "we won't send you to Juvenile Hall."

I agreed, and a short time later, I walked in the door.

"Come with me," she demanded.

I slowly followed her to the car. Moments later, we pulled up in front of Juvenile Hall. Oh no, I silently groaned. She glanced at me before suddenly turning around. Without saying a word, she drove back toward the dorm.

"I'm going to give you another chance," she said.

I glanced at her and replied, "I thought you were going to do that anyway!"

The bad attitude and aggressive behavior escalated, resulting in more fights and dissension within my life at Texas Key in Houston. I was an angry and bitter teenager, which charted my course for a brief interment at Crocket State School.

This facility was comparable to Gainesville regarding gangs and tough kids, but much worse in other areas. The rooms were high security with concrete walls and a metal bed. Each morning I was required to fold up the thin mattress from the cot and place it and the sheets beside the door. A guard removed them from the cell until bedtime that night. The only clothing allowed was a pair of britches and a shirt: no boxers or socks. A mere four bathroom breaks per day was allowed. There was a button beside the door to call for a guard when you needed to go. I was in constant trouble because my body required more frequency than four times per day, and I used the corner of my room when this happened. It was a perpetual fight in the cafeteria protecting my lunch tray or disagreements with other kids exploding into fistfights.

Weeks later, transferred to Texas Key in San Antonio, I found myself settling into a more homelike atmosphere complete with a wonderful Hispanic cook. Her enjoyment in cooking and eating good food spilled over to us kids as a true blessing. The facility rules were more relaxed with even the 'quiet room' void of a door. Residents were allowed freedom to go out on Wednesday and Saturday, which was unusual and a special privilege for unwanted and problematic teenagers. The young therapist on duty at the facility was helpful and comforting regarding communication techniques. Sadly, becoming emotionally involved with one of the kids, she lost her position as therapist and served time in jail. However, the staff truly cared about the emotional stability of the kids, and I found myself opening up old wounds in an effort to heal from within. Finally, I could not handle the flashbacks during therapy and saved my medications rather than taking them daily. I hid them in a small hole in the wall until I felt the moment I could no longer dredge up the past and look forward to the future. That day indeed arrived, and I did not want to live any longer. Although ingesting over fifty pills at one time, my attempt to end my life failed. Once again, I was put on Suicide Watch and, this time, taken to the San Antonio State Hospital for tests and evaluation. Injections of potent medication in this facility meant immediate collapse into a deep sleep. The hangover from a shot often lasted for three days before the effects wore off. A nurse or a staff member often inoculated someone due to not liking the patient or feeling intimidated by the person.

After declaring me stabilized, the system moved me to The Gulf Coast Crisis Shelter in Budda, Texas. This was a large house with a minimal number of kids, specializing in unwanted young people. It, too, had a home-like atmosphere with a Hispanic cook. Helping with the chores around the place, I considered it an honor and a lot of fun when they had me mow the yard on a riding lawn mower. We received home schooling and helped a neighbor with his emu's farm.

The first morning, we had fun gathering eggs helping him move some emus into another pen.

As the gate closed on the last big bird going into the pen, I looked at my roommate and grinned.

"This is kind of fun," I said with a chuckle.

"Yeah," he agreed. "Better than beating you at checkers again!"

I was about to argue with him when I suddenly felt something hit the side of my face.

Splat!

"Hey," I yelled at the kid. "Did you spit on me? I'll whip you. . ."

Splat!

This time a gooey wet spot appeared on his jacket.

"Hey!" he yelled. "Stop it!"

We were squaring off for a fistfight.

Splat!

Hearing a strange noise, we stopped and looked at each other then toward the noise. The owner of the farm was looking at us and laughing!

Wiping his eyes, he sputtered, "Meant to tell you boys. Them birds like to spit. It ain't that they don't like you. They are just sayin' "Thanks"."

Any desire for owning an emu farm vanished immediately!

One evening a staff member jumped on me, and I was badly beaten. Conditioned to receiving physical pain and abuse from early childhood to now, the beating did not seem out of the ordinary. However, his arrest and jail sentence surprised me. For me, harsh physical punishment was just a way of life. Following that incident, I received extra special attention to quell any threats of lawsuit. They did not realize that, for me, the beating was normal living conditions and lawsuit was not in my vocabulary!

SEVENTEEN

Six months prior to my discharge from the legal system, they returned me to Corsicanna State School. However, the facility was nothing like I remembered. Perhaps my memory played a trick on me, I silently wondered as a guard walked me down a long, cold hallway.

"This is the AIMS unit," he said. "It stands for Aggression Intervention Management."

He stopped in front of a cell door and unlocked it.

Staring at me a moment, he added, "And we do a good job of managing all kinds of aggression here."

The door swung open, revealing a stark room. The only window was a very small one in the door.

"This is where you will spend all of your time every day you are here," he said as he shut and locked the door behind me.

The man had spoken the truth. For six months, I stayed locked in that room with only my thoughts to occupy my time. I thought about my life to this point and wondered what I could have done different to make it better. I thought about Jesus and God and wondered what I had done wrong. I wondered what life was like for other people and wondered what I would do on the outside. Every kid handled AIM's Unit in their own way. Some grew angrier and lashed out. Others, like me, grew introspective, examining cause and affect. The teenager in a cell nearby spent every waking hour building his body muscles with pushups and back arms, and I wondered why. After weeks of this, his physique was lean and muscular to the point of perfection.

Throughout past years, my grandmother often made plans to bring me into her home to live with her. Each time, circumstances arose that stopped the effort. Her bouts with re-occurring shingles had played a major role in preventing several attempts. As my release from the judicial system neared, however, she readily agreed and was physically able to welcome me into her home.

Stepping over the threshold of her front door felt strangely foreign but wonderful! My life was no longer structured to when, where, why, and how to live every moment of every day. With exceptions of infrequent visits from grandparents during early years at Corsicana, I also had virtually been void of family. After settling into my room, Grandma gazed at my skimpy wardrobe. Then she smiled and shook her head.

"John, you and I are going shopping."

And shop we did! From underwear to shirts to jeans to boots, out with the old and in with the new. I felt my love and gratitude for her pour forth as she smiled and nodded her head in approval.

"My goodness, John," she murmured. "You are a fine looking young man. I am very proud of you."

I blushed and looked down at my new boots.

"Thank you, Grandma," I replied. "It sounds good to have somebody say they are proud of me."

She gently patted my arm and said, "Well, I am. And I think its time to call your dad and let him know you are here."

My heart pounded with excitement, but I murmured, "Okay." After a brief pause, I asked, "Do you think he will come to see me?"

"Of course he will," she replied as she reached for the telephone.

After talking for a few moments, she hung up the receiver and looked at me.

"Well, he can't come today, but we will check with him in a couple of days, okay?"

"Sure!" I agreed with a grin. "He's probably just real busy."

Days passed into weeks with Grandma's repeated telephone calls to my dad, but her efforts were to no avail. With each refusal to come to see me, feelings of depression deepened. Memories from the past darkened my days.

"We never wanted you in the first place!"

"Why are you here? You were not supposed to be born!"

Words echoed from deep within my mind: words lost amid beatings, accusations, heavy medications, moves, and perpetual fights for survival. For the first time in several years, I clearly visualized the faces of my mother and father, and my heart felt broken into small pieces once again.

One morning Grandma dialed the telephone. I frowned and shook my head.

"Don't try again, Grandma. It won't do any good. He doesn't want to see me."

She turned her back to me, and her voice was loud and forceful.

"If you won't come to my house to see John, Son, I don't want you coming over to see me either!"

She hung up the phone and left the room. A short time later, she left the house to go to work. Throughout the afternoon and evening I stayed in my bedroom. Alone and sinking deeper and deeper into depression, I finally stood up and walked downstairs. Methodically gathering every prescription drug to be found in the house, I returned to my room with over two hundred fifty pills of every kind in my hands. Moments later, without hesitation or regret, I ingested every pill and laid down on the bed to await blessed relief from the emotional pain of life.

"Oh, God, forgive me," I prayed. "My life has done nothing but cause trouble and hurt for everybody. I'm sorry."

My prayer continued until I succumbed to a state of unconsciousness.

EIGHTEEN

At times God reaches down, placing His Hand upon our shoulders, gracing our lives with His divine guidance. On this, my intended last night on earth, He led my grandmother to my bedside. Moments later, unable to awaken me, she telephoned the emergency response team at 911,

I regained consciousness for a short time in the ambulance and felt that I was dreaming. The vehicle stopped in the middle of the highway to transfer me into a helicopter. I later learned that I was flown from Spring, Texas, to Houston.

A short time later, in the emergency room, doctors put some kind of black stuff all over me and in my mouth. As they began pumping my stomach, everything went white ... I was above my body, looking down and watching the doctor work on me. I saw the nurses, my grandmother and my uncle standing near my body.

The doctor looked at Grandma and said, "I'm sorry Mrs. Borgstedt. He is gone. There is nothing more I can do."

Grandma yelled at him, "I am a nurse! You do not quit! I know there is still a chance."

The doctor immediately turned his attention back to my body, trying to regain a heartbeat.

My uncle, hearing the harsh demands from Grandma, walked up beside her and asked, "Is there something wrong?"

Grandma never took her eyes off the now busy doctor and quietly said, "No."

I watched him frantically work on me for perhaps a minute . . . all of a sudden, I felt myself thrust back into the inert body on the examination table with a thud. I felt my lungs fill with air and my heart start beating.

I had heard of 'out of body experiences' prior to this but chose not to believe. I do now.

Later, in ICU with closed eyes, I watched nurses, doctors, and family members come and go. I watched as someone put a plant on the windowsill. I watched them check my vital signs and administer medications. I have no explanation, reason, nor understanding for the strange, but true, phenomena. Transferred nearly two months later to the psychiatric ward, I received private and group therapy for a time.

Upon release, Grandma again took me home with her, but my grandfather and I had serious problems over my choice of music and Skoll chewing habit. Watching a music channel one afternoon in my bedroom, he burst into the room with a sledgehammer. Seconds later, my television was shattered into jagged pieces.

"John, I told you," he shouted, "I don't like you listening to that kind of music!"

He glanced around the room and saw my Skoll can sitting on the dresser. Grabbing it, he threw the can at me.

"And I don't like you chewing this stuff!" I told you your great granddad died from lip cancer, and I'm not going to allow it in my house!"

The violent outburst pushed me over the edge . . . it was fight or flight. Choosing the latter, I ran from the house without any extra clothes, my medications, or plans for where I might go. Walking aimlessly through the streets of Houston, by late evening I was hungry and tired. Watching restaurants and donut shops closing for the night, I saw them throwing unsold food into their dumpsters. As they left for the night, I ate the edible discards. Sleeping quarters that night was a park bench. On this, my first night as a homeless person, I found that survival is possible. Thus, this was my lifestyle for a short time.

One chilly night I found a patio restaurant closed and decided to sleep there. I found a mop head for a pillow and pulled a tablecloth off one of the tables to use for a blanket.

A short time after laying down, I began having a seizure. Without the needed medication, the seizures became more frequent and severe. Sometime later, the police found me in serious condition and had me transported to a hospital for treatment. Upon recovery, my grandmother once again took me home with her.

Approaching age eighteen and knowing in my heart that my presence was both pain-filled and stressful, I soon left and moved in with a teacher friend who had worked at Corsicana. The structured life in various hospitals and incarceration facilities had not prepared me for life in the real world. Perhaps the lessons learned to date were better suited for living a life of hand-to-hand combat in a war zone! The result was poor choices: the wrong crowd, fighting, and stealing, which eventually led to distributing and selling weapons on the black market. With an income of sixteen to seventeen thousand dollars in my pocket following each transaction and no concept of the 'wrong' path, I began training a down and out acquaintance to work with me.

One evening while in route to Waco with another arms delivery, this pattern of criminal activity exploded into serious and life-threatening consequences. Unaware that my partner had not paid for gas at a service station where we had filled, I drove into Waco with the black market items in the back seat and trunk of the car. Apparently feeling bulletproof as we pulled up to the security shack of an apartment complex, he retrieved the British 303 from the back and fired a gunshot into the air.

"That was a dumb move!" I growled as I shoved the car in reverse and sped from the parking lot. Racing through the streets of Waco, I knew that we had to get out of sight fast or face serious criminal charges. Adrenalin from fear and dread coursed through my veins as the sound of sirens and the flash from blinking lights filled the night sky. Within moments, law enforcement from local, county, and state troopers surrounded our car as helicopters circled overhead. Soon they removed us from the car and unloaded the two boxes of dynamite sticks, tasers, British 303's, SKS, sawed-off pump, handguns, and jewelry. Handcuffed and sitting beside me on the ground, my partner looked at the interrogating officer and shook his head.

"This stuff all belongs to my dad," he said. "We weren't doing anything wrong."

"Well," the officer replied slowly, "you two just sit tight while we run a numbers check for stolen property."

My heart pounded as the officer walked back to his patrol car and radioed for needed information. After a short time, he returned with unexpected but welcome news for us.

"None of these serial numbers have been reported stolen. You are free to go." He paused a moment before adding, "Don't let me catch you firing another gun within the city limits of Waco. Understand?"

"Yes, Sir," I said. "We won't. That was a dumb thing to do."

Although avoiding further questioning that night, three days later, police issued arrest warrants against us. My life was again in the hands of the legal system, and I was destined to learn adult consequences for illegal and immoral behavior.

NINETEEN

The county issuing the warrant against me was out of the jurisdiction of my residence at the time. Thus, officials requested that I meet them at the county line to turn myself in for resolution. With my long and numerous record of run-ins with the law, fear of the unknown was not among my emotions as I was handcuffed and put in the back seat of a patrol car.

The following morning from jail, I telephoned the owner of the house where I was living. My bedroom was located in the back section of her residence. Her voice sounded tense and guarded as she answered the phone. She listened in silence as I told the reason for my absence. I heard her take a deep breath before responding.

"You are better off than you would have been at home last night," she said firmly. "Someone threw a brick through the living room window and then shot your bedroom full of holes. Your mattress. Your pillow. The walls. If you had been home last night, John Borgstedt, you would be dead! No doubt about it."

Shock sent the blood rushing through my body. Visions of gunfire slicing through the night into my bedroom seemed like a scene from a movie. Things like this don't happen in real life!

My hands were shaking as I hung up the phone. Slowly returning to my cell and sinking down onto the cot, I held my head with both hands and rocked back and forth.

"Oh, God," I quietly murmured over and over. "Oh, God, thank You. You have saved my life again, and I don't know why. Thank You, God. Thank You."

A short time later, the defensive fight regarding my case began. Although a mere eighteen years of age, I was an old warrior in the ways of the legal system. Plea bargaining began soon after arraignment. My defense attorney was no help as we sat down at the bargaining table. With my competency to withstand a jury trial in question, I looked at the prosecutors and crossed my arms over my chest. Let the games begin, I thought grimly. I'm not that little ten-year-old boy at the mercy of my mother now.

A prosecuting attorney looked down at the open file on the desk. Then he peered at me over his glasses.

After clearing his throat, he stated, "Mr. Borgstedt, you have a healthy rap sheet for as young as you are." He glanced at the defense attorney and then turned his attention back to me.

"Your partner has stated in writing that you are the arms dealer. He is nothing more than a victim of poor judgment in choosing friends. Agree to a forty five year prison term, and we can settle this case right here and now."

Before my attorney could reply, I said, "No deal!"

This was to be the first offer of many.

"Thirty five years, Mr. Borgstedt."

"No."

Later, "Twenty five years, Mr. Borgstedt."

"No!"

And soon after that, "Our final offer is twenty years, Mr. Borgstedt. I suggest you take the offer while it is still on the table!"

"No!" I replied.

Following the latest plea bargain, I sank into depths of despair. About eighteen months had lapsed with me sitting in a jail cell, looking at additional years confined within walls of a prison. My life was nothing but pain, heartache, and a bleak future of more incarceration. I was tired of the fight and did not want to live anymore. Relief would only come with death. Attempts with overdosing in the past had failed. I silently vowed that I would not fail this time!

Although I was seriously determined to take my own life, God did not agree. After guards found me unconscious, hanging by my neck in the cell, I was sent to Vernon State Hospital, a facility for the criminally insane, for tests and evaluation.

The question was, "Is this eighteen-year-old male with a history of bad choices competent enough to withstand a jury trial?"

The doctors at Vernon State Hospital listened intently as I unfolded my life story openly and honestly before them. The sessions were long and grueling as I relived old painful memories from my home to the never-ending list of facilities and hospitals. I told them of the unspeakable abuse by my mother, the horrors witnessed and experienced during hospital confinements, and the ongoing pain of abandonment.

Upon completion of tests and evaluations, the results stunned the prosecuting attorneys.

"John Borgstedt is not mentally capable of withstanding a trial."

"What?" the attorney gasped. "What do you mean 'not mentally capable of withstanding trial'? He didn't have any problems here!"

"Well," the doctor said slowly, "that is confidential between doctor and patient. But, if you want to take him to trial, I guarantee with one hundred percent accuracy, he is not competent to stand trial."

The diagnosis of "incompetent to stand trial" translated into eminent release from Vernon State Hospital due to the statute of limitations running out. Thus, soon an assistant to the District Attorney arrived. His demeanor was friendly and straight to the point.

"Look," he said quietly, "This is what we're willing to do. Five years incarceration in the state penitentiary."

"No," I replied.

My defense attorney, summoned to explain the benefits in this offer, sat down beside me.

"John," he said. "I think you better take the five years the state has offered. You will go to prison, but your time in jail up to this point will count as time already served."

With a brief nod of my head, I said, "Where do I sign?"

TWENTY

With a five-year prison sentence hanging over my head, I sat in jail awaiting transport into the Texas prison system. Nearly two years had passed since my arrest. In the county jail, confined with other convicted men awaiting transport, I wondered and worried about life in prison. Witnessing horrors of hatred, torture of child molesters, stabbings, and constantly fighting for personal belongings were normal living in this jail. I could only imagine how bad life would be in prison. It was already apparent this incarceration was different then any I had previously experienced. I often asked, "Do you think I can make it there?"

My heart pounded with dread with the arrival of the prison bus one morning. Even the transporting of prisoners was different then any I had experienced before. From jailhouse orange jumpsuits to prison whites and hands and feet shackled around the waist, forewarned me of things to come. Only then did they lead us to the bus for the trip to the prison. Even the transporting of prisoners was different then any I had experienced before. The only sound was the rustle of chains as we got on the bus and sat down. No one spoke. No one moved. Similar to the quiet before a raging storm, silence hung in the air like a death sentence over the busload of convicts. The bus stayed off main highways, rather taking back roads every mile of the way.

Texas Department of Corrections
John Borgstedt   TDCJ ID# 837915

Unlike most, I was already conditioned in survival training, as we became the property of the Texas Department of Corrections. Similar to a tortured animal, my reflex against possible danger was immediate without thought to consequence. As the bus neared the prison, I accepted the fact that I would be fighting for my life until release.

Upon arrival at the transit Gurney Unit, one hundred fifty men lined up, buck naked, as guards searched every inch of our bodies for weapons and contraband. After physical evaluations, photographs, the shaving of our heads, and dousing in white powder, guards showered us with lye soap and water to kill any bugs we may have brought into the facility.

While awaiting classification, we stayed in a large dormitory. The huge room contained fifty or fifty-one bunk beds with full view of showers and commodes. There was no privacy at any time from fellow prisoners or officials. I saw things happen continually that I did not want to see. But this was my life for the following six months. At times sent into the fields to 'chop dirt' with hoes, we sang songs, making up our own lyrics. Problems between prisoners were often settled in fistfights out in the field with field officers betting on the outcome. This occurred only with the permission given by the officers.

Classification options included Trustee, Minimum, or Medium with most of the decision based on previous incarceration. While in the Gurney Unit, I received Medium Custody. However, after aggressive fighting and numerous write-ups on disciplinary reports, I was transferred to the Conley Unit with a Closed Custody classification.

The Conley Unit was 96% gang related, which included some officers with gang affiliation. Again, I was in the minority, and survival, both physical and mental, required the will, wit, and wisdom to fight until death in any given situation.

One afternoon a gang of blacks decided to jump me. Although outnumbered, I fought a long and hard battle. By the time the fight was broken up, a laceration on my head required five stitches and four more under one eye.

Leaving the infirmary a short time later, I walked back into the room and stood on one of the tables.

"If anybody else is ready to go again, lets do it. We'll get it over with right now!"

There were no takers, but I never let my guard down again. Life here was the survival of the fittest, and any sign of weakness was not an option.

Young prisoners brought in for petty crimes hung themselves rather than becoming a victim of rape by gang members. Even broom handles were used as weapons of torture when a gang member inserted it anally into a co-prisoner. If a gang member from one race spoke to a member of an opposite race, it was a death sentence against the offender. Drugs and contraband were plentiful and prevalent, entering the prison by the hands of corrupt officers. Despicable acts against humanity were daily occurrences in the Conley Unit. I was an aggressor and attacker if anyone even acted as though they were going to cross me. Any prisoner put in my house was fair game as far as I was concerned, and I beat him down, regardless of the consequence. After one year of fighting for life and against the system, I was again transferred.

The Segregation Unit was a twenty-four hour per day lockdown. Prisoners were supposed to be allowed one hour per day recreation, but, most times, officers allowed this only at their discretion. Rebellious prisoners, which I definitely was, seldom received recreational privileges, and numerous times missed meals. My rage and insubordinate attitude, although conditioned and understandable, kept me on the path of self-destruction. One year later, I, once again, was moved . . . this time to a Maximum Security prison near Amarillo. This newly constructed facility housed the worst of the bad.

As I entered the gates of the Bill Clemens State Penitentiary, I was unaware of the fact that sunlight, grass, and sky were no longer a part of my life. They existed merely in my memory.

This facility was state of the art in maximum security. Cameras positioned to view prisoners from every angle were everywhere throughout the facility. There were no windows in this unit, and merely diffused sunlight entered the interior of the building. This minimal amount of filtered light granted me the opportunity of knowing it was daytime. My whole world was a sparse, windowless cell. Officers passed all meals, medical supplies, and personal needs through a slot or 'bean' hole to me. There was no physical contact unless my rage erupted in physical violence. When this happened five officers in riot suits responded, throwing percussion grenades into my house and spraying pepper gas. Once inside, they stripped me of my clothes and beat me. After removing all of the bedding, they left me in the cell naked for weeks at a time. The price paid for rebellion in Bill Clemens was indeed high both physically and emotionally, and, for two years, I survived and paid my debt to society in Bill Clemens Penitentiary.

TWENTY ONE

With shackles securely positioned on my feet, hands, and around my waist, the cell door opened.

"Let's go," the gruff voice of an officer demanded.

As always, my body was like a coiled spring while walking between and ahead of the armed guards. For five long years, I had fought and survived for this one day in time, and now nothing seemed real. The sounds of life within the cellblock faded into the distance as we left Bill Clemens and entered the Wall Unit. Within a short time, normal civilian clothes replaced the shackles and prison whites. With my discharge papers and a one way bus ticket to Houston in hand and one hundred dollars in my pocket, I walked past officers and guards toward the entrance doors of the prison. After stepping through the gates into freedom, I felt my body weaken and grow numb with shock. I had not been out of the confines of bars and bare walls in five long and grueling years. The purity of sunlight and the expanse of the sky overhead seemed heavenly! For a long moment, I was unable to breathe, staring in absolute awe of the world I had long ago forgotten. The air felt clean and fresh, and the old familiar scent of dirt and grass brought a smile to my face and song in my heart. Slowly absorbing the awesome beauty of the open sky, the grass, and the vastness of the world, I felt the Almighty Power of God erasing the anger and pain from the past.

Within the blink of an eye, the huge weight of aggression, bitterness, and animalistic instinct for survival vanished. For the first time in my life, I felt safe and totally liberated. In that moment, God filled my heart with gratitude, hope, joy, peace, and love.

I fell to my knees. Touching the plush green grass, I laughed and tossed blades of the precious greenery into my mouth. The childlike impulse granted me the sweet taste of life. I laughed and stood to my feet. Squaring my shoulders, I realized, for the first time in my twenty-two years, I was truly free! No longer bound by the cruel custodial control of my mother, hospitals, institutions, court system, or halls of justice, for the first time in my life, I was void of bondage!

While riding the bus to Houston, I gazed out of the window like a small child, drinking in the awesome wonders of the world. I will never take the sky or clouds for granted again! I silently vowed. I will cherish every day, giving thanks to God for the grass, trees, birds, and critters!

Suddenly my heart felt the loving touch of God. A miracle unfolded as Jesus cleansed my heart with absolute forgiveness of past pain and suffering. The dark and devastating venom of ill will poured forth from my soul, purifying my very existence as miles passed beneath the bus. This was indeed the first day of the rest of my life!

Twenty two-years within a structured, harsh disciplined life had taught me survival of the fittest; however, lessons learned inside were useless to me in my new average daily living environment. My background of violence and rage-induced existence taught me nothing about common social skills, employment principles, or healthy relationships. Therefore, several times, I found myself involved in unstable situations testing my resolve to avoid physical confrontations. By the grace of God, the use of brute force was no longer my solution to every problem and first line of defense. I quite often found myself walking away at the slightest hint of an upcoming volatile situation. Thus, I began a new journey on a straight path toward a healthy, happy horizon of possibilities.

The day arrived when visions of siblings faces returned with clarity, bringing a kindred yearning into my heart to see them once again. Until this moment, thoughts of my family remained buried beneath pain and a lifetime of battling for survival. All communication had ceased after a lack of response to my letters over the years. Re-uniting would be a challenge since losing my grandmother who had passed away during my interment in prison.

One afternoon I saw a beautiful butterfly glide downward and land on a leaf. I smiled and stood perfectly still as it left the leaf and soared toward me. As it landed on my shoulder, gently flapping its beautiful wings, I thought, perhaps this is a sign from Grandmother. She loved butterflies. The memory of the little blanket that she had made for me when I was a small child returned. Adorned with hundreds of butterflies, the precious cover provided the healing love needed at the time. Now, I chuckled with pleasure at the remembrance. The butterfly gracefully lifted off my shoulder and disappeared into the heavens. Perhaps, I thought, now is the time to try locating my family. I murmured softly, "Thank you, Grandmother. I love you, and I will find them."

And, indeed, I did find my father and siblings via the internet. Although rightfully concerned about re-uniting with a brother who had spent time in prison, my sister and I established a loving and working relationship.

After corresponding via email for a time, I learned that, since our early childhood, my mother had warmed my siblings about allowing me into their lives.

"Your brother is going to get out one of these days. And when he does, he is going to kill you. He is going to kill me. He is going to ruin our lives!"

She had not given them the letters and cards that I had sent over the years, and the result was a deep-rooted fear and mistrust of my motives for locating them. Trust is an earned gift from a loved one, and proof of sincerity would only come with the passage of time.

Thus about two years later, it came to pass that my sister and I approached the house of my mother. Awaiting a response to our knock at the door, I suddenly felt like that ten-year-old kid standing in the courtroom. My heart pounded with excitement as the door opened. My stepfather graciously invited us inside.

"Your mother isn't here right now," he said. "Come on in. She should be back before long."

While awaiting her return, we looked at old family photographs and talked about days gone by. Most pictures of me were taken within the confines of the numerous hospitals and institutions, but the visual remembrance did not produce anger in me. I was no longer fighting for acceptance or seeking lost childhood. My heart, mind, and soul were indeed at peace with the past.

Suddenly the back door opened and my mother entered the house. As her gaze shifted from my sister to me, she stopped walking and stared. Her face seemed void of emotion.

I smiled and quietly said, "Hello, Mom."

As I slowly walked toward her, she did not move a muscle nor blink her eyes. I knew my presence must be a shock. Her small boy of ten was now twenty four-years-old, six feet five inches tall, and weighed nearly three hundred pounds.

Gently hugging her close to me, I said

"I love you, Mom." Pausing momentarily, I added, "And I forgive you."

A second later, without a return hug or saying one word, she stepped away from me and turned toward the door. Without a backward glance, she walked out of the house and closed the door. A moment later, we heard her car backing from the driveway.

For the first time in my life, abandonment and rejection by my mother did not hurt. Embracing the teachings of Jesus, I granted her my love and forgiveness. I am at peace with my past and spiritually motivated to greet each new sunrise with honor, dignity, and gratitude.

Thank You, my Lord God Almighty, for healing the broken heart of this little lost boy.

I lean back in the office chair and gaze at the littered desktop. Stacks of paper filled with typewritten words seem to stare back at me.

"Done," I murmured.

The low, unimpressive comment echoed within the silence of the office. I yawn and stretch before turning my attention back to the computer. Perusing the last sentence written, my hands suddenly begin to tremble.

"It's done." I repeat in a slightly louder voice. "My life story is told. After all of these years, it is finally untangled and written!"

Tears flow down my face as I look around the room. Although spending hours, days, and months in this office, I truly see the contents and upheaval in normal living for the first time.

My mind returns to long solitary hours in this room researching, studying documentation, writing and re-writing.

I notice a half-eaten sandwich and half-empty cup of cold coffee setting on a corner of the desk. Knowing my wife Virginia had brought it, I now wonder if I even acknowledged her thoughtful gesture, let alone thanked her. A low groan of regret and gratitude blends with the sound of my boots pacing back and forth on the office floor. For the first time since starting this journey into a dark past, I truly see and appreciate her calm and loving wisdom dispelling fear, doubt, and defeat in moments of weakness. Numerous nights of horror-filled remembrance surfaced during sleep, and I awakened from nightmares to her gentle, loving voice calling me back into the present. My gaze shifts upward.

"Thank You, sweet Jesus, for my Virginia. You could not have graced my life with a greater gift." I chuckle and add, "But I guess You already know that. Thank You."

Suddenly the door to the office opens, and Virginia quietly walks into the room; her eyes clouded with concern.

"John," she says quietly. "Are you okay? I heard you talking, and . . ."

I grab her and hold her in my arms.

In a whisper, I murmur, "Great. Just great! My autobiography is written."

I feel her body tremble with excitement. She steps away and starts pacing. I stare at her for a moment before asking, "What's wrong?"

"Nothing," she replies. "Now its time for you to go to work."

"Work?" I sputter. "What do you mean ' go to work'? I've been working!"

Turning to face me, she puts her hands on her hips.

"Now you start helping other kids, remember? That is your destiny, John, and you know it. Now you start spreading the word to help other little ones. Expose the truth of mental and physical abuse to the powers that be. Counsel kids in bad situations and . . . "

My laughter of total agreement interrupts her recital of my personal goals. The glow of success from finishing a tough job disappears as visions of my future Boys Ranch returns in a tidal wave of optimism and ambition.

Minutes later, wife Virginia and I leave our home, slowly walking hand in hand into the late evening. A horse knickers in the distance, and we look at one another and smile. Our hearts and minds are as one.

Although a childhood of pain, neglect, deception, and cruelty, I stand before you today a strong and determined man with a compassionate heart and high moral standards. This literary exposure of scars is but the first step of a journey to greater purpose; awareness and action.

I, John C. Borgstedt, hereby dedicate my life to the restoration of the emotional and physical well-being of the lost, battered, and bruised. By the grace of God, perhaps my humble effort of love will prevent a small boy from ever feeling the need to declare, "I Love You, Mom. Please don't break my heart . . ."

Key Note:

For additional information on having John speak for your group, please write us or visit our web site at:

John Borgstedt
P.O. Box 1201
Canton, Texas 75103
www.iloveyoumom.net

CPSIA information can be obtained
at www.ICGtesting.com
Printed in the USA
FFOW04n0653190916
27778FF